Fast Break

Great Basketball of the 20th Century

Mel Cebulash

New Readers Press

New Readers Press wishes to thank
Naismith Memorial Basketball Hall of Fame
for its help in producing this book.
Wayne Patterson, Research Specialist

Copyright © 1993
New Readers Press
Publishing Division of Laubach Literacy International
Box 131, Syracuse, New York 13210-0131

Printed in the United States of America

Photo credit:
Page 37 Houston Chronicle;
all others AP/WIDE WORLD PHOTOS

9 8 7 6 5 4 3 2 1

Library of Congress Cataloging-in-Publication Data

Cebulash, Mel.
Fast break : great basketball of the 20th century /
Mel Cebulash.
p. cm.
ISBN 0-88336-744-0
1. Basketball—United States—History.
2. Basketball players—United States. I. Title.
[GV885.7.C42 1993]
796.323'0973—dc20   93-6897
                                                      CIP

Contents

Introduction

In the 1950s, the school yards in Union City, New Jersey were always filled with kids after school.

Basketball was the favorite game at Washington school yard. The two baskets in the school yard stood side by side. So only half-court games were played. Usually, the games were three-on-three.

One basket was known as the "good" basket. It had a "kind" rim, letting backboard shots fall in most of the time. The rim on the other basket (the "bad" basket) seemed higher and kicked shots out most of the time.

A new kid in the neighborhood could easily spot the good basket. Bigger kids (high school age) used the good basket, and *it* had a net (some of the time).

I played on the bad basket along with the other kids who went to Washington School and St. Augustine. We all knew we'd get to play on the good basket when we reached high school age.

Playing on the bad basket had its advantages. Sometimes the bigger kids didn't have enough players. So they picked a kid playing on the bad basket court and let him play with them. Being "good enough" to play with bigger kids was quite an honor—almost like going to the pros!

One afternoon, I was picked by Johnny Mareno. He told the other big guys I was good enough.

If I remember right, I missed two shots before another big guy showed up, sending me back to the bad basket. Still, that short game was an honor this kid never forgot.

No doubt, the great stars in this book once played in school yards, too. Except when they got to high school, they got "picked" to play indoors.

—Mel Cebulash

The Scoring Guard

Bob Cousy starred in college basketball for Holy Cross. In 1950, the Boston Celtics signed him to play guard.

At 6 feet, 1 inch, Cousy wasn't expected to be an NBA star. Boston just wanted him to move the ball up the court. Then the tall men could take over. In those days, NBA scoring leaders were centers and forwards.

Bob Cousy averaged 4.9 assists per game during the 1950–51 season. In fact, he was fourth in the league in assists. He also scored an average of 15.6 points per game.

Boston fans liked Cousy's playing style. He led the team into fast breaks. He tried fancy passes, and they worked. He also tried some fancy shots, and they went in. He was a thrilling player to watch.

The Celtics finished second in the Eastern Conference for the 1950–51 season. The year before, Boston had finished last. Much of the credit went to Ed Macauley, the Celtics' new center, who had scored over 20 points per game. Yet some fans figured the real credit belonged to Cousy.

In 1951–52, Cousy's play delighted basketball fans. The way he handled the ball amazed players and fans. Sometimes Cousy fooled other Celtics with his fancy no-look passes.

Cousy jumped to second place in the NBA in assists for 1951–52. He scored over 21 points a game, making him third in the league. He was named to the All-NBA first team. "The Couz" was becoming a big star!

The Celtics were set to play Syracuse in the playoffs. Syracuse won 47 games and finished in second place in the Eastern Conference in 1952–53. The Celtics won 46 games and dropped into third place. Still, Boston fans figured their team would get by Syracuse in the playoffs.

Syracuse fans had other ideas. The Syracuse Nationals (known as "The Nats") were a tough team. They'd always won in an opening series of the playoffs. On the other hand, Boston had *never* won in an opening series.

The first game in the three-game series was played in Syracuse. To the surprise of Nats fans, the Celtics won 87–81.

The series then moved to Boston. The Celtics needed one more win to make the second round of playoffs. The Nats needed two wins in a row.

Fighting hard, the Nats led at halftime, 42–40. Boston battled back, to the delight of the huge crowd. After three quarters, Boston led 62–59.

The Nats came back in the last quarter. With seconds left to play, Syracuse led 77–76.

Cousy got the ball. A Syracuse player immediately fouled Bob Cousy. He went to the foul line for one shot.

At best, Cousy could tie the game. If he missed the foul shot, the game was over.

The heat was on Cousy. He set himself and shot the foul. The ball went up and in! The score was tied. The teams had to play a five-minute overtime period.

The close play continued. With seconds left in the overtime period, Cousy again went to the foul line. His shot tied the score at 86–86. So the teams got ready for another five minutes of overtime play.

In the second overtime, both teams tried to slow the play and wait for a clear shot. There was no 24-second clock rule in those days. So teams often held the ball for minutes at a time without shooting.

Again, Cousy scored the last overtime basket. This time, the shot was a field goal, locking the score at 90–90.

The third overtime started. The scoring went back and forth. A Syracuse basket gave the Nats a 99–97 lead. The clock showed about 10 seconds left to play.

The pass-in went to Bob Cousy. He dribbled upcourt. Time was running out!

Cousy fired a long one-handed shot. It went in—clean! The score was tied at 99–99 as time ran out.

Bob Cousy, number 14, drives past the Syracuse defense to score in the Eastern Conference Finals.

The Nats scored five straight points to start off the fourth overtime. Boston fans grew quiet. With Syracuse ahead 104–99, the Celtics were in big trouble.

Bob Cousy was far from through. He scored five points in a row. The Celtics and Nats were tied again.

At every turn, Syracuse ran into Cousy. He stole the ball as Boston fans cheered him on. He scored foul shots. He got the ball again. He scored more foul shots. The Celtics had a four-point lead!

In the end, the Celtics won 111–105! Boston had scored 21 points altogether in the last two overtimes. Cousy made 17 of those points!

Fans cheered Bob Cousy's outstanding game. In all, he scored 50 points. Cousy even made 30 out of 32 foul shots!

Boston didn't win the NBA Championship that year. After beating Syracuse, the Celtics lost out in the Eastern Division Finals to the New York Knicks.

Overall, Bob Cousy starred for 13 seasons with the Celtics. With Cousy leading them, Boston won six NBA Championships.

Cousy averaged over 18 points a game in his pro basketball career. Teams feared his long one-handed shot. The teams also feared his passing. He ended his playing days with 6,955 assists.

Bob Cousy could dribble, shoot, and pass. For a shorter player, he could even jump. He was an all-around all-star. In 1970, Cousy became a member of the Basketball Hall of Fame.

Basketball's Giant

Wilt Chamberlain played college basketball at the University of Kansas. He left school to play with the Harlem Globetrotters.

He played with the Globetrotters for one year. Then he went on to sign with the Philadelphia Warriors for the 1959–60 season.

Wilt Chamberlain had grown up in Philadelphia. Fans remembered him from his high school days. They welcomed him back. The fans expected the Warriors to be a much better team with Chamberlain playing for them.

Years before, Chamberlain had been given the nickname "Wilt the Stilt." The name stuck, but it really no longer fit Chamberlain. He was tall. He stood 7 feet, 1 inch. But he wasn't thin. He weighed close to 275 pounds. Wilt Chamberlain was big—and powerful.

NBA players quickly learned about Chamberlain's great strength. He bulled his way inside and took down rebounds. By the end of the season, he was the league leader in rebounds. He averaged 27 rebounds per game.

Chamberlain also showed he could score baskets. He scored 37.6 points per game, which put him on top of the league.

Because of his outstanding play, Chamberlain won the Rookie of the Year award for the 1959–60 season. He was also voted Most Valuable Player in the NBA. *And* he was named the NBA All-Star game's MVP. He was the first player in history to win all of these titles in one season.

In the All-Star game, Chamberlain led the Eastern team to a 125–115 victory over the West. He scored 23 points and led both teams in rebounds.

Chamberlain's scoring average went to 38.4 points per game for the 1960–61 season. His rebounding was better, too. In one game against the Boston Celtics, he set an NBA record with 55 rebounds. His amazing record for rebounds in one game still stands!

For two years in a row, Wilt Chamberlain led the NBA in scoring and rebounding. Philadelphia fans expected another great season from Chamberlain in 1961–62. He probably gave the fans even more than they expected.

As soon as the season started, Chamberlain jumped off to a lead in scoring. In December, he set an NBA scoring record. He made 78 points in a game against Los Angeles.

In January of 1962, Chamberlain scored over 70 points again! This time, he hit for 73 points in a game with Chicago.

Chamberlain continued his great scoring. By the end of February, he had scored 60 or more points in each of 15 games. Wilt Chamberlain had become a scoring machine.

On March 2, Chamberlain led his team onto the court at Hershey, Pennsylvania. The Philadelphia Warriors were giving people in Hershey a chance to see NBA basketball. The New York Knicks played the Warriors that Saturday night. Hershey was known for the chocolate treats made there. Now, the 4,124 people who came to the game were in for another kind of treat.

In the first minutes of play, the Warriors jumped off to a big lead. Wilt Chamberlain scored over and over again. He had 23 points when the first quarter ended. Philadelphia led 42–26.

Chamberlain's scoring didn't surprise the fans in Hershey. They knew how well he had been playing all year. His foul-shooting did surprise the fans, though. He usually hit on 6 out of 10 foul shots. But after one quarter in Hershey, he hadn't missed a single foul shot. He'd hit nine straight!

In the second quarter, the Knicks fought back. They cut Philadelphia's lead. The

Knicks even held down Chamberlain's scoring. He only made 18 points, giving him 41 for the half. He also missed a foul shot after hitting 10 straight. The Warriors led 79–68.

The game turned into a battle between the Knicks and Wilt Chamberlain. At times, three Knicks covered Chamberlain, hoping to stop the big Warrior center. He still fought them off and scored. His 28-point quarter raised his game total to 69. The Warriors led 125–106.

Wilt Chamberlain seemed like a safe bet to break his own NBA record of 78 points scored in one game. He only needed 10 points. The fans

Wilt Chamberlain sinks the basket that gave him 100 points in a single game. The record still stands.

in Hershey cheered for him as the fourth quarter started.

By then the Knicks probably expected to lose. Still, they didn't want to give the game away. They also didn't want to give Chamberlain a new scoring record. So they tried hard to rally.

The Knicks just couldn't stop Wilt Chamberlain. The night seemed to belong to him. With 46 seconds left in the game, he scored his thirty-sixth field goal. With that shot Wilt Chamberlain had scored 100 points for the game!

Fans raced onto the court. They wanted to touch him, to shake his hand. He finished the game with exactly 100 points because the clock ran out while the fans were still on the court. He might have scored even more in the last 46 seconds of the game. The Warriors won 169–147.

Wilt Chamberlain's 100-point game remains an amazing NBA record. In setting the record, he made 28 of his 32 foul shots. He also made 36 field goals for 63 tries.

At the end of the 1960–61 season, Wilt Chamberlain's scoring average stood at

50.4 points per game. His average also stands as an amazing NBA record.

In all, Wilt Chamberlain played NBA basketball for 14 seasons. During that time, he set many records in scoring and in rebounding. He was voted into the Basketball Hall of Fame in 1978.

Chamberlain's 100-point game was probably his best ever. The fans in Hershey thought so.

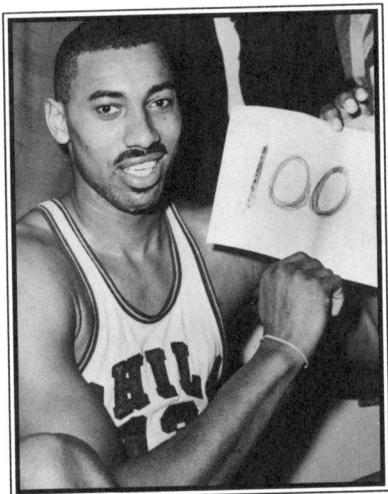

The 100-point man celebrates.

Made
of Steel

His name was Lew Alcindor. He starred in college basketball at UCLA. He was 7 feet, 2 inches tall, and he played center.

After college, Alcindor signed to play with the Milwaukee Bucks during the 1969–70 season. The Bucks had finished last in the Eastern Conference in 1968–69. They expected to be much better with Alcindor on the team.

Alcindor proved to be as good as expected. Milwaukee moved up to second place in the Eastern Conference. Alcindor scored an average of 28.8 points per game.

He was named NBA Rookie of the Year for the 1969–70 season.

With a year of pro play behind him, Alcindor became the league leader in scoring in 1970–71. Over the year, he averaged 31.7 points per game.

Alcindor was picked as the Most Valuable Player in the NBA for 1970–71. After the regular season, he led the Bucks to their first and only NBA Championship.

Later in 1971, Alcindor surprised sports fans. He had joined the Islamic religion a few years earlier. "Now," the tall basketball star said, "I am taking a new name. I am Kareem Abdul-Jabbar."

So, in a way, the Milwaukee Bucks had a new center for the 1971–72 season. His full name was Kareem Abdul-Jabbar. Fans quickly started calling him Kareem. Newspapers started listing him as Abdul-Jabbar in their box scores of Milwaukee games.

Playing like champions, the Bucks got off to a good start in 1971–72. They won 25 out of their first 28 games.

On December 10, 1971, over 10,000 Milwaukee fans came out to see the Bucks go against the Boston Celtics. The Celtics were leading their division, so Milwaukee fans expected a tough battle.

Boston started fast. They jumped off to a 9-point lead early in the quarter. The Bucks battled back and cut Boston's big lead. Still, the quarter ended with the Celtics on top 28–26.

The second quarter started out like a replay of the first quarter. Boston again jumped ahead by nine points. Milwaukee answered with a string of baskets. Soon Boston's big lead was gone again. By halftime, the Bucks led 52–50.

The third quarter belonged to Kareem Abdul-Jabbar. With Milwaukee fans cheering him on, Kareem fired in basket after basket. Nicknamed "the sky hook," Abdul-Jabbar's long hook shot thrilled the fans.

Abdul-Jabbar hit on jump shots. He rebounded. He dropped in layup shots. The Celtics couldn't stop him!

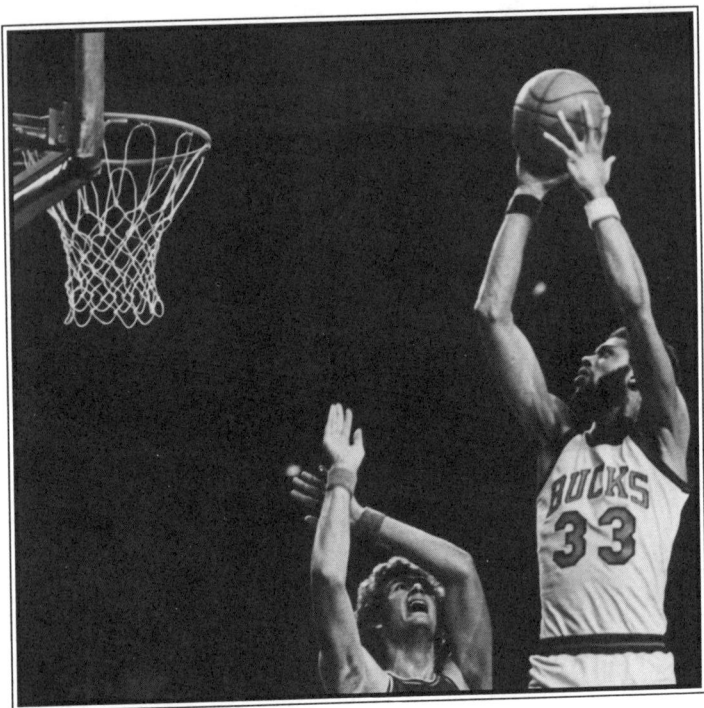

Kareem Abdul-Jabbar, the NBA's all-time total scoring champion

By the end of the quarter, the game seemed out of reach for Boston. The Bucks led 85–70. Kareem had scored 18 points in the third quarter.

Milwaukee fans wanted more scoring from Abdul-Jabbar. They wanted him to go after his one-game record of 53 points. "Shoot!" they called when he got the ball.

Near the end of the game, Abdul-Jabbar tied his one-game record. The fans stood and cheered him on. They wanted to see a new record.

When the game ended, Kareem Abdul-Jabbar had scored 55 points! He also had 17 rebounds. The Bucks won 120–104.

Kareem's record 55 points also set the Milwaukee record for scoring in one game.

By the end of the season, Kareem's 2,822 points also set a new one-year scoring record for the Bucks.

Kareem Abdul-Jabbar led the NBA in 1970–71 with an average of 34.8 points scored per game. For the second year in a row, Abdul-Jabbar was named as the NBA's Most Valuable Player.

Two seasons later, he won the Most Valuable Player honor again. The Bucks weren't as lucky. They lost the 1973–74 Championship Series to the Celtics.

Abdul-Jabbar was traded to Los Angeles before the 1975–76 season. He'd grown up in New York City. Yet because of his years at UCLA, he'd come to think of Los Angeles as home. Abdul-Jabbar was happy to be a Laker.

The Lakers were happy, too. Kareem Abdul-Jabbar won his fourth Most Valuable Player award in his first season with Los Angeles. For the 1975–76 season, Abdul-Jabbar added another first place to his NBA record. This time, he led the league with 1,383 rebounds.

After seven years of hard play in the NBA, Kareem Abdul-Jabbar showed no signs of tiring. Still, he was almost 30 years old. Some Los Angeles fans figured the team might need a new center soon.

He fooled these fans and lots of other people. He played better than ever in the years that followed. He won the Most Valuable Player award two more times, giving him the NBA record with a total of six MVP awards.

Abdul-Jabbar's playing days ended in 1989. He was 41 years of age and had starred in the NBA for 20 years. He truly seemed to be made of steel.

Kareem's 55-point game still stands as a Milwaukee record. Yet it may be broken. One-game records are often broken.

Kareem's league records may never be broken, though. He scored 38,387 points. He played in 1,560 games. He even holds the record for 4,657 personal fouls.

The NBA may *never* see another player like Kareem Abdul-Jabbar. In his 20 years, he played over 57,000 minutes. He is sure to become a member of the Basketball Hall of Fame. In fact, he probably earned a place in the Hall of Fame while he was with Milwaukee. He was one of the greatest ever!

The Pistol of Basketball

Pete Maravich played his college basketball at Louisiana State University. For three years in a row, Maravich was picked for All-American honors.

Maravich was a 6-foot, 5-inch guard. His shooting was so good that he broke all college scoring records. In three college seasons, Maravich ended with a career average of 44.2 points per game.

Because of his speed at scoring baskets, Maravich picked up a nickname. He became known as "Pistol Pete."

The nickname fit Maravich well. He blasted shots into the basket, especially long shots. He could also fire off perfect passes!

Along with his shooting and passing, Pistol Pete had amazing skill at handling the basketball. Pete Maravich dribbling a basketball was a show in itself.

After college, Maravich signed to play with the Atlanta Hawks for the 1970–71 season. The Hawks had one of the best teams in the NBA. Most Atlanta fans were thrilled by the news about the signing of the great Pete Maravich. Still, some fans wanted to wait and see. They weren't sure Pistol Pete would help the team.

The Hawks didn't improve in the 1970–71 season. Maravich wasn't at fault. With his passing, he quickly showed he was a team player. The team just needed to get used to his style of play.

With his shooting, Pistol Pete also showed the other NBA teams how he got his nickname. For the season, he averaged 23.2 points per game. He was named to the NBA All-Rookie team.

Maravich was ill when the 1971–72 season started. An infection kept him out of action for a couple of weeks. After that, he started slowly. Still, he averaged 19.3 points a game for the season.

The following year, Pistol Pete was healthy again. He averaged over 26 points a game for the season. He also jumped to sixth place in the league with 546 assists.

Maravich's average went to 27.7 per game for the 1973–74 season. He was second only to 6-foot, 9-inch Bob McAdo in scoring. When it came to scoring, Pistol Pete was a giant.

After the season, Maravich was traded to a new NBA team—the New Orleans Jazz. New Orleans didn't expect to have a winning team in their first year. They still expected to draw big crowds. They had a player who had starred in Atlanta—Pistol Pete Maravich.

New Orleans fans cheered Pistol Pete during the 1974–75 season. They didn't have many other reasons to cheer. The Jazz only won 23 games.

Maravich played well even though the team was terrible. His scoring average dropped, but his 6.2 assists per game were good enough to place fifth in the NBA.

The Jazz won a total of 38 games during the 1975–76 season. They weren't a great team, but they were getting better.

Pistol Pete averaged 25.9 points a game for the season. He probably wished he was with a winning team. But the Jazz had improved—enough to finish ahead of Atlanta.

The Jazz weren't any better in 1976–77. Pete Maravich couldn't be blamed. He played hard—all the time.

On February 25, 1977, the New York Knicks played the Jazz in New Orleans. Over 11,000 fans came out for the game. Both teams had losing records. Many fans probably just wanted to see Pistol Pete.

In the first quarter, Maravich led the Jazz to a 31–26 lead. Still, the game didn't start off as a great one for Pistol Pete. He missed a few easy shots.

By halftime, the Jazz led 65–43. Pete Maravich wasn't missing any easy shots now. In fact, he wasn't missing many shots at all. Jazz fans cheered Maravich as the team went off the court for the break.

Earlier in the season, Pistol Pete had scored 51 points in a game. Those 51 points were the most he had ever scored in an NBA game.

Pistol Pete topped 51 points in the third quarter. When the quarter ended, the Jazz led 96–77.

The Jazz were going to win. The fans knew that. They still stayed on. They loved the way Pistol Pete was shooting.

With a little more than a minute left in the game, Maravich fouled out. He had 68 points. No guard had ever scored 68 points in an NBA game. The fans cheered Maravich's record-breaking game as the Jazz won 124–107.

When the 1976–77 season ended, Pistol Pete was on top of the NBA in scoring with a 31.1 average.

Knee injuries kept Pistol Pete out of action for part of the next two seasons. He averaged over 20 points in each of the seasons. Still, the knee trouble spelled the end for Pistol Pete Maravich.

Pistol Pete Maravich, the high-scoring guard of the
New Orleans Jazz, in the game of his career

In the 1979–80 season, the Jazz traded Pete Maravich to Boston. Pistol Pete finished the year with the Celtics. For the season, he averaged 13.7 points for 43 games. After 10 years of play, Pistol Pete Maravich's playing days were over.

In January of 1988, Pete Maravich died of a heart attack in Pasadena, California. He'd passed out while playing a little game of basketball with some friends at a local church. He was 40 years old.

Two years earlier, Pistol Pete Maravich was named to the Basketball Hall of Fame. And, many of his college scoring records still have not been broken.

The Rocket Fires

Calvin Murphy played college basketball at Niagara University. During that time, Murphy was one of the top scorers in the country. He was named to All-American teams for three straight years.

When Murphy graduated, his NBA future was not assured. Most NBA teams thought Calvin Murphy was too short for pro ball. He stood 5 feet, 9 inches.

Murphy wasn't worried about his size. He'd played against bigger guys all through college. He usually was the high scorer in his college games. Sometimes, he even grabbed the most rebounds. Murphy figured all he needed was a chance with the pros.

The San Diego Rockets liked what they saw. They decided to give him that chance. Calvin Murphy was signed to play with the Rockets in 1970–71.

After a few games, the Rockets knew they hadn't made a mistake. Murphy was shorter than the players he faced, but he was also faster. Murphy could fake and shoot past any player guarding him. Often, Murphy could outjump the player, too. Calvin Murphy definitely belonged in the pros.

At the end of the season, Murphy was picked for the NBA All-Rookie team. The other guard picked for the team was 6-foot, 5-inch Pistol Pete Maravich.

The following year, the Rockets moved to Houston. For the 1971–72 season, Murphy averaged 18.2 points a game. He made 89 percent of his free throws, and that was good enough for second place in the NBA.

Over the next three seasons, Murphy continued his great play at guard. He also

Hall of Famer Calvin Murphy (number 23) leaps between larger players to hook another shot in.

continued as one of the best free-throw shooters in the NBA.

Murphy scored an average of 21 points a game during the 1975–76 season. His great foul shooting got better, too. He reached 91 percent, making 372 out of 410 foul shots. That placed him second in the league.

The 1977–78 season marked Murphy's eighth year in the NBA. He still had his speed. He moved like a rocket. Yet he seemed to be the only rocket on the Houston Rockets.

On March 18, 1978, the New Jersey Nets lined up against the Rockets in Houston. A little over 6,000 people came out for the game. The Rockets were in last place. They'd lost 10 games in a row.

Coming into this game, Murphy had scored 27 foul shots without a miss. He hoped to keep the run going. Houston fans came to cheer him on.

At halftime, the Rockets led 58–53. Murphy still hadn't missed a foul shot! He'd scored 32 points already! Houston fans cheered for Calvin Murphy.

The Nets battled back in the third quarter. They held Murphy to four points. Still he didn't miss a foul shot. Houston led 78–77.

In the last quarter, Houston fans got a few surprises. After making 36 straight free throws, Calvin Murphy missed one. In fact, he missed three foul shots in the last quarter!

Murphy only made 9 out of 12 free throws for this game. Houston fans shook their heads. They couldn't remember a game when Calvin Murphy had made only 75 percent of his free throws.

The Nets won the game in the last minute of play, 106–104. For the Rockets, the loss was their eleventh in a row.

Even though the Rockets lost, Houston fans stood and cheered. Calvin Murphy had missed some free throws in the game. But he scored 21 points in the last quarter, giving him 57 for the game! His 57-point total was a new Rockets record. The little guard was amazing!

Murphy also scored 24 out of 40 field goals, which meant he was hitting on 60 percent of his in-play shots.

Murphy finished the 1977–78 season with an average of 25.6 points a game. He hit 92 percent of his free throws, making him second in the league.

Two years later, Murphy set an NBA record for free throws made. He scored 206 of 215 free throws during the 1980–81 season. At last, he was first in the league! His 95.8 foul-shot average was also first. He broke the old NBA record for highest percentage of foul shots made!

Before he quit playing, Murphy led the NBA in free-throw percentage two more times. Murphy ended his playing days like the star he was. He led the league by hitting on 92 percent of his free throws during 1982–83.

Calvin Murphy had started his playing days with a question mark hanging over him. In no time at all, he showed he was big enough for the NBA.

Murphy's 57-point game still stands as the Rockets record. His 17,949 points also stand as a Rockets record, along with his 4,402 assists.

Murphy's 2,103 rebounds are no record. Still, they tell a lot about the way Calvin Murphy played basketball. He figured he was big enough to play—and to go under the basket, too. To prove it, he grabbed more than a few rebounds. In 1993, Calvin Murphy was elected to the Basketball Hall of Fame.

Murphy played in the NBA for a total of 13 years. After Murphy's time, other short players came into the league. Of course, they had to be good. But their size was no longer a question. Calvin Murphy had answered that question—for all time.

Larry Bird Flies High

The Boston Celtics won only 29 games in the 1978–79 season. Still, the Celtics had some good news about the future. A great college star from Indiana State had signed on for the 1979–80 season. The star's name was Larry Bird.

Boston fans welcomed the high-scoring forward from Indiana. They figured Larry Bird could really help the Celtics.

The fans were right about Bird. He averaged 21.3 points a game in his rookie year. As a result, he was named Rookie of the Year.

With 61 wins, Boston finished the 1979–80 season in first place. They lost in the playoffs. But the Celtics had come a long way from last place.

Larry Bird averaged over 21 points a game again during the 1980–81 season. He also pulled down 10.9 rebounds a game, making him fourth in the NBA.

In the playoffs, Bird also averaged over 21 points a game. The Celtics beat Houston in the Finals for the 1980–81 NBA title.

At 6 feet, 9 inches, Larry Bird handled the basketball as well as any guard. He rebounded as well as many centers. His passing and shooting were outstanding. Many people thought of him as the best all-around forward in the NBA.

In 1981–82, Bird won another title. This time, he was named Most Valuable Player of the All-Star game.

As the years passed, Larry Bird seemed to get better. He made the 1983–84 All-NBA team for the fifth year in a row. To top that, he was named the league's Most Valuable Player for the season.

The Celtics went on to win another NBA Championship in 1983–84. Led by Bird, Boston took the title in a series with the

Lakers. Bird averaged 27.5 points a game and was voted Most Valuable Player for the playoffs.

The next season, Larry Bird surprised basketball fans with an even better season. This time, he added three-point shooting to the many things he could do well.

On March 13, 1985, Boston went to New Orleans. The Celtics were playing the Atlanta Hawks.

Hoping to draw big crowds, the Hawks had scheduled 12 games in New Orleans that season. For the first nine games, the Hawks hadn't pulled in many fans.

So the Hawks may have been surprised to find a sellout crowd at the game. Over 10,000 basketball fans were on hand. The fans' cheering helped to explain things. They were there to see the Celtics, especially Bird and the Celtics' forward, Kevin McHale.

Nine days earlier, Larry Bird's one-game Celtics scoring record of 53 points had been broken. Kevin McHale had set a new Boston record with 56 points.

In New Orleans, the Celtics jumped into an early lead. By the end of the quarter, Larry Bird had 12 points, and Boston led 35–27.

Bird scored 11 more points in the second quarter. He had 23 points for the half, and the Celtics were ahead 65–58.

The Hawks came back early in the third quarter. After a few minutes of play, Atlanta tied the score at 69 each.

With the crowd cheering, the Celtics fed the ball to Larry Bird. Bird hit one basket after another. He drove in for two points! He fired up a long jump shot! He hit his free throws! He couldn't be stopped!

In all, Bird scored 19 points in the third quarter. Much of the time, the Hawks had two men on him. Still Bird scored! He ended the quarter with 42 points for the game. Boston led 100–89.

The Hawks played hard in the last quarter. Still, Atlanta couldn't dent Boston's big lead. With less than two minutes left in the game, the Hawks were behind by 10 points.

Larry Bird had 49 points. A technical foul was called against Atlanta. The Celtics sent Bird to the line. He made the free throw—his fiftieth point of the game!

Seconds later, Bird hit a long jump shot. The crowd cheered. He was closing in on the Boston one-game scoring record. Not much time was left—probably not enough time.

With less than a minute left to play, Bird scored another basket. He had 54 points!

The Hawks scored. The Celtics quickly got the ball to Bird. He was fouled and went to the line for two shots.

Bird hit both free throws, bringing his game total to 56. He'd tied McHale's record! Time was running out.

Seconds later, a whistle sounded just as Bird fired off a three-point shot. It went in! The crowd went wild!

Wait! The whistle came before the shot! The shot didn't count. Bird had two free throws to shoot.

As the crowd cheered, Bird hit both foul shots. He had 58 points.

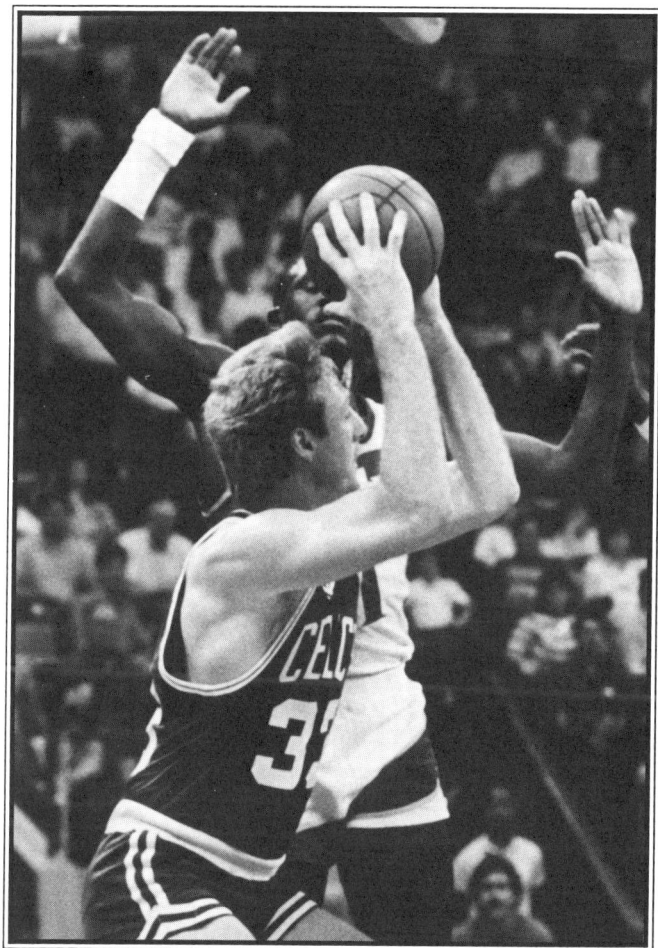

Larry Bird tries to get past the Hawks' Dominique Wilkins on his way to a 60-point game.

An Atlanta three-point shot went in. The ball went to Bird. He missed a three-point shot. McHale grabbed the rebound with only a few seconds left. He passed the ball out to Bird.

Bird got off a shot. The buzzer sounded. The shot went in! He had a record 60 points! The Celtics won 126–115.

Larry Bird starred with the Celtics for 13 years. Near the end, he battled against back injuries much of the time. He played for the United States Olympic basketball team in 1992. The team became known as the "Dream Team." At 35, Bird was the oldest member of the great U.S. team that easily won the gold medal.

Always Magic

Earvin Johnson played college basketball at Michigan State. In 1979, Johnson signed with the Los Angeles Lakers. By then, Johnson had become a great star in college basketball. He'd also picked up the nickname "Magic."

6-foot, 8-inch Magic Johnson played at guard and forward spots for the Lakers during the 1979–80 season. He quickly showed L.A. fans that his nickname fit him.

Johnson could shoot, dribble, and rebound like a champion. Best of all, his passes worked like magic. By the end of the season, Magic Johnson was seventh in assists in the league.

49

Magic really put on a show in the last game of the NBA finals. Replacing an injured Kareem Abdul-Jabbar, Johnson started at center and scored 42 points. The Lakers won the NBA Championship, and Magic Johnson was named Most Valuable Player for the playoffs.

Magic missed half of the 1980–81 season because of a knee injury. When he came back, he seemed as good as ever. So L.A. fans looked forward to Magic's next full season.

Magic again saved his best tricks for the playoffs in 1981–82. Playing guard, he averaged 11.3 rebounds a game in the playoffs. He scored 17.4 points a game and got 9.3 assists.

For the 1981–82 season, the Lakers once more won the NBA Championship. For his all-around play, Magic was again named Most Valuable Player for the playoffs.

Johnson became the passing star of the NBA in 1982–83. He led the league with 10.5 assists a game. In the playoffs, his assists jumped to 12.8 a game.

As the seasons passed, fans all over enjoyed seeing Magic in action. His big

Magic Johnson (right) punches the ball away from Kevin McHale of the Boston Celtics.

smile seemed just right for the tricks he did with a basketball—or with *getting* the ball. Along with his assists, he also became known for his skill at stealing the ball.

Magic lifted his scoring to 23.9 points a game during the 1986–87 season. He also

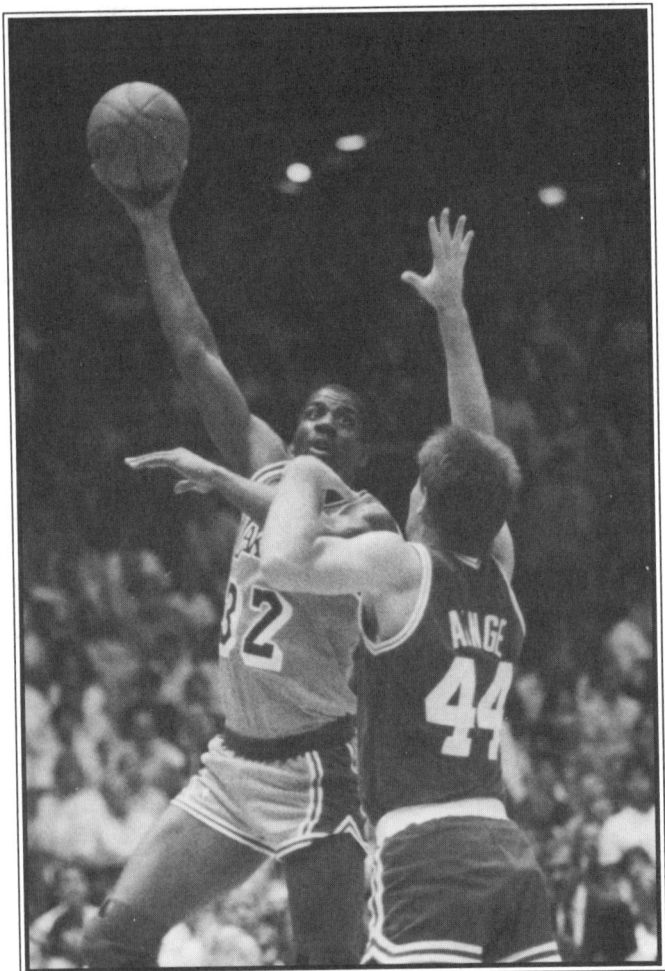

Johnson shows his skill at shooting with a sky hook in the NBA Championship game.

led the NBA in assists with 12.2 assists per game. He was named the Most Valuable Player in the NBA that season.

In the playoffs, Magic led the Lakers into the Finals against the Boston Celtics. The first two games in the Championship Series were scheduled for play in Los Angeles.

The Lakers won the first game 126–113. They also won the second game 141–122. L.A. fans figured their team was on their way to a championship.

The Finals moved to Boston for the next three games. The Celtics had a great record playing at home, so they expected to do better.

With Boston fans cheering them on, the Celtics took Game Three 109–103. They weren't through yet!

Close to 15,000 people filled Boston Garden for Game Four. Most of the people were Boston fans. They cheered the Celtics on to a 29–22 lead after the first quarter.

When the first half ended, Magic led L.A. scoring with 19 points. Still, Boston fans were happy. Their Celtics led 55–47.

The L.A. fans in the crowd had little to cheer about in the third quarter. The Lakers couldn't cut into Boston's lead. The quarter ended with the Celtics leading 85–78.

The Lakers were down but not out. They tied the score halfway through the last quarter.

With their hometown fans roaring, the Celtics jumped ahead once more. They led 103–97. The clock showed less than two minutes left to play.

Suddenly the Lakers stole the ball! A three-point shot went in. Boston's lead was cut to 103–100!

A pass got away from a Celtic and bounced out of bounds. L.A. ball! The clock showed a minute left. A Laker made a jump shot! The Celtics' lead was down to one point!

Boston missed a shot. The Lakers rebounded. The ball went over to Magic. He fired a long pass down the court. Kareem Abdul-Jabbar, the L.A. center, leapt up. He took the pass and slammed it through the net for two points! The Lakers led 104–103!

The clock showed about 15 seconds left to play. A Boston pass went to Larry Bird, their great forward. He fired up a long shot. The shot was good for three points!

The Celtics led by two points.

An L.A. free throw cut the lead to one point. The second foul shot missed, but the ball went out of bounds. L.A. ball! Five seconds left to play!

Magic passes the ball to teammate Byron Scott.

Magic Johnson had scored only eight points in the second half. He hadn't even scored in the last quarter. Still, the pass came to him. The Lakers needed some magic.

Johnson threw up a hook shot. Two seconds left! The ball went in! The Lakers led 107–106.

The Celtics missed a long shot as unhappy Boston fans watched. The game was over! Once more, Magic Johnson had lived up to his nickname.

The Lakers went on to win the NBA Championship for 1986–87. For his great play, Magic Johnson was voted Most Valuable Player for the playoffs.

Magic Johnson's great pro career ended in November of 1991. He decided to retire because he found out that he had the HIV virus. Later that year, he played in the All-Star game and won the Most Valuable Player award. He also was a member of the United States Olympic "Dream Team," that won the 1992 gold medal. As always—he was Magic.

The King at Work

Michael Jordan starred in college basketball at North Carolina. He left college early to play with the Chicago Bulls.

Jordan's first NBA season was 1984–85. The Bulls expected a lot from Jordan. He gave them more than they expected.

Michael Jordan won the Rookie of the Year award for 1984–85. He was third in the NBA in scoring with an average of 28.2 points a game.

Shortly after the 1985–86 season started, Jordan broke a bone in his foot. The season was almost over when he came back. He was still able to break an NBA scoring record. In a playoff game against

Boston, he scored a record 63 points. The old record of 61 points had been set in a 1962 playoff game.

At 6 feet, 6 inches, Jordan was shorter than many guards in the NBA. Yet he could jump higher than many centers in the league. He also had a special driving skill. When Jordan went up on a drive for the basket, he could keep himself in the air longer than any player in the NBA. He could wait to shoot until after the man guarding him fell off.

With his driving skill, his speed, and his great outside shooting, Michael Jordan was almost impossible to stop during the 1986–87 season. He led the league with an average of 37.1 points a game. Some teams even tried putting two men on him. As a result, Jordan also led the NBA in free throws taken during the season.

Jordan's 35-point average gave him the NBA scoring title for 1987–88. He also put his speed and quick hands to work for another first-place honor. He led the league with an average of 3.16 steals a game. For his play, he was named the league's Most Valuable Player for the season.

As a team, the Bulls were getting better. The Bulls started to add good players to help Michael Jordan. Chicago fans began to think they might have a championship team in the works.

Some fans worried that Jordan wouldn't fit into a championship team. They thought he wasn't a team player.

The fans who questioned Jordan's team play learned a lesson during the 1988–89 season. Jordan again won the scoring title with an average of 32.5 points a game. He also passed a lot—when it counted. For the season, he averaged 8.0 assists a game, which made him tenth best in the NBA.

Chicago played well during the 1989–90 season. On March 28, 1990, the Bulls were in Cleveland to play the Cavaliers.

Jordan came into the game with a league-leading average of 33 points a game. To win the game, the Cavaliers knew they needed to stop Michael Jordan.

After one quarter of play, the Bulls led 27–26. The Cavaliers hadn't stopped Jordan. He had 16 points.

The Bulls pulled to a 53–50 lead at halftime. Jordan scored 15 more points, giving him a halftime total of 31.

Jordan's shooting in the third quarter amazed Cleveland fans. He couldn't seem to miss. In all, he scored 20 points. He had 51 for the game, and the Bulls led 89–78.

The Cavaliers thrilled their fans in the fourth quarter. The Cleveland team fought back. With seconds left to play, the Cavaliers tied the score at 105–105!

The ball came to Michael Jordan. He'd scored 10 points in the quarter. He had 61 points in the game!

Jordan tried a jump shot. The big crowd watched as Jordan's shot, the last shot of the quarter, moved toward the basket. The ball went in and out! Jordan missed! The game was going into overtime play!

The missed shot didn't bother Jordan. He made up for it as soon as overtime started. He hit a jump shot.

Michael Jordan lofts a shot in as Cleveland's
Mark Price tries, in vain, to stop him.

Jordan lets loose his trademark tongue as he racks up 69 points for a career record.

The Bulls went ahead and stayed ahead through the overtime. When it was over, Chicago won 117–113. The great Michael Jordan had scored his all-time high of 69 points! He'd also hit another personal high with 18 rebounds.

Jordan was named Most Valuable Player for the 1990–91 season. The following season, he led the Bulls to an NBA Championship. After the championship games, he was named Most Valuable Player for the playoffs.

Michael Jordan took home his sixth straight scoring title in 1991–92. He also won his third Most Valuable Player title. Chicago had won its first NBA title!

The next season, the Bulls took home their second straight NBA Championship. Once more Michael Jordan was named Most Valuable Player for the playoffs.

Following the season, Jordan joined Magic Johnson, Larry Bird, and other American basketball stars on the 1992 United States Olympic "Dream Team."

The U.S. played eight games and won the gold medal in basketball for 1992.

Michael Jordan's gold medal was his second Olympic medal. He'd won a gold medal as a member of the U.S. Olympic basketball team in 1984.

When the 1992–93 season started, Michael Jordan still looked and played like a young star. Before the season ended, Jordan reached the age of 30. But he also topped 20,000 career points. It was clear he was going to be around for a long time.